I love reading

# Scary Snakes
## by Monica Hughes

**Editorial consultant: Mitch Cronick**

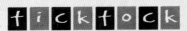
ticktock

**We would like to thank: Shirley Bickler and Suzanne Baker**

ISBN 1 86007 042 6 pbk
Printed in China

Picture credits
t=top, b=bottom, c=centre, l-left, r=right, OFC= outside front cover
FLPA: 18-19. Shutterstock: 10-11, 14, 20t. Superstock: OFC, 7, 8, 15, 16-17.
ticktock photography: OFC, 4, 5, 6, 12, 13, 14-15c, 20b, 21.

# CONTENTS

Words that look **bold like this** are in the glossary.

# Meet the snakes

Snakes are found almost everywhere, but very few are **poisonous**.

They have a dry, scaly skin.

As the snake grows its skin gets too small for its body.

The snake **sheds** its skin in one long piece. A new skin is underneath!

**Scaly skin**

4

Snakes don't have eyelids so they can't blink.
They sleep with their eyes open.

Snakes have a
tongue shaped
like a Y.

# Snake babies

Some snakes lay eggs.

Their eggs are soft and leathery, not hard like a bird's egg.

Snakes lay their eggs in a hole in the ground or in a **mound** of leaves.

Corn snake

When a baby snake is ready to **hatch** it cuts its way out of the egg.

6

It uses a special egg-tooth to do this.

Some snakes do not lay eggs.

They give birth to baby snakes.

Anaconda snake

8

Scaly skin

# King cobras

The king cobra is the longest poisonous snake in the world. It can be five metres long.

King cobras live in thick forests in South Asia.

They hunt and eat birds, rats and snakes. They spit poison at their **prey**.

King cobras lay eggs in a nest of leaves and twigs.

Baby snakes hatch after about 60 days.

# Adders

Adders are also known as vipers.

They live in Europe and Asia in forests and on **grasslands**.

Adders eat rats and lizards.
They chase their prey or **ambush** it.

Adders give birth to as many as
20 baby snakes at one time.

11

# Royal pythons

This snake lives on grasslands and in forests in Africa.

It eats small animals like rats and gerbils.

The royal python grabs its prey. Then it wraps its body around the prey and squeezes it to death.

The female snake lays eggs in an underground **burrow** or between rocks.

She keeps the eggs warm and the babies hatch after 10 to 12 weeks.

# Rattlesnakes

Rattlesnakes live in hot deserts.

They eat birds and small animals like rats and mice.

They bite their prey with poisonous **fangs**.

Fangs

Rattlesnakes have hard scales at the end of their tails.

When the snake rattles the scales it sounds like marbles in a tin.

Rattlesnakes give birth to baby snakes.

Y shaped tongue

15

# Anacondas

Anacondas live in South America.

They are the heaviest snakes in the world.

Anacondas eat pigs and deer.

They hide in shallow water and ambush their prey. They wrap their body around the prey and squeeze it to death.

Anaconda

**Y shaped tongue**

Anacondas give birth to baby snakes.

The babies can swim when they are a few hours old.

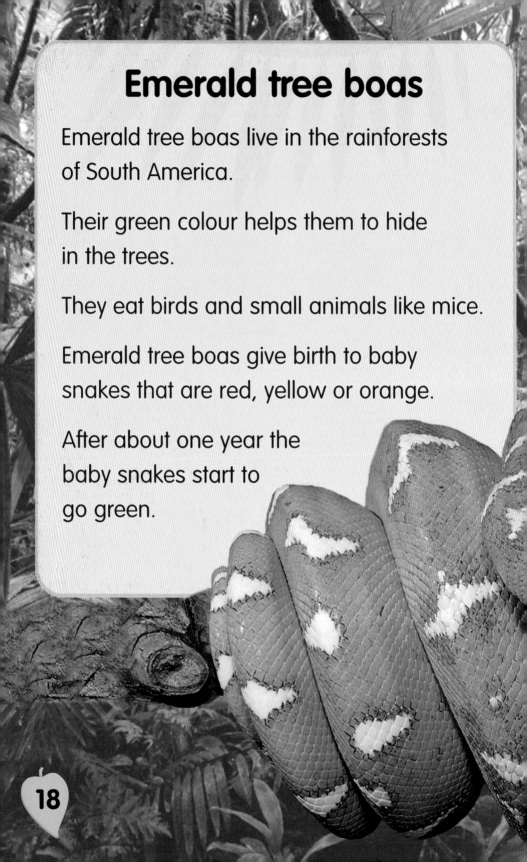

# Emerald tree boas

Emerald tree boas live in the rainforests of South America.

Their green colour helps them to hide in the trees.

They eat birds and small animals like mice.

Emerald tree boas give birth to baby snakes that are red, yellow or orange.

After about one year the baby snakes start to go green.

Baby emerald tree boa

# Corn snakes

Corn snakes live in America.

They live up trees and hide in buildings and under rocks.

They are not poisonous and make good pets.

Corn snakes eat rats and mice, so they are useful on farms.

Y shaped tongue

Corn snakes lay
as many as 25
eggs at a time.

Baby snakes
hatch after
60 days.

**Scaly skin**

# Thinking and talking about snakes

What happens when a snake gets too big for its skin?

How does a royal python kill its prey?

Why is green a good colour for emerald tree boas?

22

How long can a king cobra grow to?

Which snake would you least like to come face to face with?

Would you like to have a pet corn snake? Why?

# Glossary

**ambush**
To hide and then attack!

**burrow**
An animal's home that is hidden away.

**fangs**
Long, sharp teeth.

**grasslands**
Hot, dry places with lots of grass and only a few trees.

**hatch**
To come out of an egg.

**mound**
A heap or a pile.

**poisonous**
Something that can hurt or kill people, animals or plants.

**prey**
An animal that is hunted by another animal for food.

**sheds**
Gets rid of.